Windows

Presented to:

my Beloved Chris

By:

Ron

February 14, 19 87

For

Larry, Leah, Lucas, Mark

And most of all

For Carl

Who is patient still

Windows

By

Martha Oliver Williams

Photography by Lee Angle

BROWNLOW PUBLISHING COMPANY, INC.
P. O. Box 3141
Fort Worth, Texas 76105

Brownlow Gift Books

Flowers That Never Fade

Flowers of Friendship

Flowers for You

Flowers for Mother

A Father's World

Better Than Medicine — A Merry Heart

Making the Most of Life — From A to Z

A Time to Laugh — Or Grandpa Was a Preacher

Thoughts of Gold in Words of Silver

With the Good Shepherd

Living With the Psalms

The Story of Jesus

For Love's Sake

Today Is Mine

Windows

Daybreak

Peace Be With You

The More Years the More Sunshine

University of Hard Knocks

The Longfellow Birthday Book

By His Side — A Woman's Place

Aesop's Fables

Contents

Part Three: Windows to the Soul

Part Four: Windows to Life

Part Five: Windows to Yesterday

Windows

My words are windows to my heart

And soul.

If they are dark

And streaked with dirt,

I am not seeing clearly

The beauty of my world;

Nor can you see

The whit of goodness,

If only by reason of Creation,

That is within me.

Whatsoever Things Are Lovely

When the turmoil of all the world around,

Or the bitterness

Of some disappointing association,

Or a lonely, hateful time

Presses down upon my spirit,

And brings a sickness to my heart,

I enter into the quiet of my mind

And remember.

I remember lovely things and chordant sounds

Stored there.

And there comes a healing.

Must there be a depth for every height?

When fingertips are touching

Stars,

Must there be a fall?

Must there be?

Ah, but I can bear the depths

As long as there are heights

And stars

To reach again.

The sky is bluer from lofty heights.

The mountain tops, unsurmountable

Before,

Become as rocks beneath my feet.

Clouds,

Whether real,

Or those that want to close about my spirit,

Drift by below,

Beyond the reach to threaten me.

The universe is smiling,

And so am I.

If only I could teach my heart

To stay

On mountain tops.

Heart's Capacity

Sometimes it seems that my heart

Has not the capacity

To hold the love I feel,

Nor the reach to encompass,

With loving warmth,

The ones who are dear to me.

So I can only try to touch the heart of each,

In its own way and need,

One at a time.

Because

I am not happy because you love me,

Not this alone,

My contentment reaches to encompass friends;

Those who need me,

And supply my need for understanding;

To children who honor

And love me;

To my Lord who supplies my hungry soul.

But my awareness and capacity for these

Are far greater

Because you love me.

Empty Offering

To offer love,

Selfishly,

Because of self evaluation

Of loveliness,

Is an empty offering and not love at all.

But love given freely

Full of selfless charm and grace

Fills a life and satisfies

The heart.

Hopeful Patience

Anger has clouded your mind

And closed your face

In cold darkness.

But I remember your face full of love.

So I wait.

Surely

It will be so again.

Prisoner of Shadows

My shadowed state of mind
Makes prisoner of all the lovely thoughts,
And beautiful words,
That might be written
For you.

Reaching for the Wind

Love
Will not be grasped,
Nor held against the will.
It's like reaching for the wind,
And finding nothing in your hand
But emptiness.

A Corner of Your Need

You must,

As do I at times,

Need the reassuring touch

Of a comforting hand,

Or loving word,

To calm disquieting unrest.

So

I will supply the corner of your need

Assigned to me,

My friend.

Love Is Gone

When love goes,

It is not with stealthy tip-a-toe.

But rather walks with steady

Stride

Pushed by barbs and cutting words.

Then with clanging noise

Of bitter hurt,

The door is closed behind

With never a returning.

Love is gone.

Forgive me

For never loving you in the way of lovers.

My heart could not tune to yours

In the ecstacy of lover's passion,

But rather reached for you

In tenderness of rarest of friendship,

Woman to man.

A Time for Renewing

Sometimes,

It seems, there are no words to say;

My soul has no song to sing.

Then it is a time for renewing;

A time to look with my eyes upon a quiet wood;

A city street, busy with the lives of men;

Or time to listen with my ears and heart

To a symphony,

Or to a simple melody;

Or to hear quiet voices

Murmuring words of love and goodness;

Or time to look to understand words

From the greatness of man;

To contemplate the Word

From the perfect Goodness of God.

These surely will renew again

The spring of songs and words

Within me.

An Appeal

When I am sad and dark

In spirit,

It's then I need to have you touch my heart

In gentleness,

So I may know again

Assuredly

That you love me.

An Echo of a Song

Some hearts never tune to togetherness.

Some, though once tuned

Only sing

A muted echo of a song.

Even now we stand

Touching,

Saying words,

But yet, it seems that I can hear

An echo.

To My Son's Pregnant Wife

I remember.

I see the look of wonder,

Shared,

But private, closely held,

Upon your face,

And in your eyes,

Revealing this new dimension of womanhood

Within you.

One generation removed,

The source of my own private wonder.

I remember.

A Baby Comes Home

A home

Enfolds its heart

Around

A new-born baby

And becomes

Complete.

For Lucas, Five Days Old

Sometimes

We can pick you up when you fall,

But not always.

Sometimes

We can make things right for you that go wrong,

But not always.

May God grant us wisdom to teach you

To stand and do,

And to be a man.

To a Christian

It really doesn't matter

If I do not know your name.

I need only know

Our kindred minds.

I need only know the love we share in Him

Because He first loved us

And wills us to be

One.

Surcease

My soul

In humility, kneels at the cross.

I weep.

Whether war of soul and will

Over unquiet desires,

Or bitter repentance, I search to know,

And fail.

But warring self, or contrition,

At the Cross

I find surcease.

Mastery

The purity in my soul

Cries for ascendancy

In the face of conspiring evil,

The goodness in my heart

Would overflow to inundate

The dark desires that threaten me.

May God help me keep in liberation

This part of me

That He would own.

Reparation

There is no going back,

No re-creation of innocence.

The stain of guilt

From wounding words rashly spoken;

From things hastily done

Stays upon the consciousness.

Though there is no complete forgetfulness,

There is absolution

At the mercy seat of God.

Traps and Snares

Thoughts,

And words of beauty and peace,

And deeds of kindness

Are trapped inside the snares

Of anxiousness

And doubt

Laid by ourselves.

Lord, lift my cross

By laying Yours upon my life,

And free my soul

To serenity.

Life

When all my life is gone,

The seventy years that due,

I will have lived with love

Because of you — and you.

So while a part of youth

Is yet of mine to live,

Let me touch your hand

With what is mine to give.

And if I bring you joy

By word, or act, or smile,

My three score years and ten

Will all have been worth while.

Growing Old

My eyes despise the look of aging flesh.

I cringe,

And draw back my soul in blind retreat

At thoughts of halting steps

And failing eyes.

I must teach myself to look at others, older,

And see beyond deterioration;

To see the graceful blooming of mellow wisdom,

Kindness and greater love;

To learn that growing old is but God's own way

Of recreating child-like souls

To live with Him.

I must teach myself these things,

For time is racing swiftly

Through my three score and ten;

My lot, too, God willing,

Will be a growing old.

A Beautiful Life

A beautiful life is made,

Not left to happenstance.

Each word of kindness,

Each thoughtful deed

Is painted into the work of art

Called living.

Entanglement

To tangle the heart

In the life and love of another

Is like a knotted cord,

Impossible to quickly pull away

And separate.

Only concentration on untangling

With patient care, can keep the cords,

Or be it very lives,

Unbroken.

My friends are as rare editions

Of books,

Each a single copy made.

They must not be left upon the shelf

Untouched,

If I would learn of life,

And love

From their depth.

I must read

And handle each with loving care,

And they will bring me

Joy.

Seeking

I reach for fulfillment of dreams,

And find elusiveness.

Even reality becomes unknown.

Surely I am what I seem,

Or perhaps

I'm only yet to be.

But this I apprehend,

Reach I must,

And in my reaching I am,

And I will be.

Wasted Hours

Hours

Passing like low flying clouds on a stormy day,

Hurrying nowhere,

And disappearing into the darkness of the time,

Fill my days and rob my soul of contentment.

Moments spent alone

In the quiet of the night,

Rebuild the will to face another day,

Should it too be a day

Of vain and fallow hours.

A Certain Knowledge

Time lifts its feet

In a swiftly running pace

Toward a dreaded time,

While mind and heart hang in limbo,

Uncertain,

Uncreative, senses dulled

By the knowing of the certain parting;

Then you will be gone

With frustrating finality.

A Narrow Vision Space

When I look out my window space,

I see but such a limitation

Of God's creation.

A patch of blue and living green,

Scarcely marred by broken, bent decay.

A pleasant, lazy look, unanswerable.

Just so, I find myself

With narrow view of God's own image,

Man.

Choosing not to see too much

Of broken life and rotted soul,

Lest I'm compelled

To step without my vision space

To reach with heart and hand

To share the load of those who need me.

On a Daughter's Pain

Tear filled eyes and anguish stricken face

Of this beloved extension of me,

Turns to me confidently, for relief.

How can I offer ease,

When the brunt of her pain has struck

Within my inner being,

With no relief

Until her tears are dried?

Lord, grant me wisdom to know,

And to teach her,

How to live with pain

When it comes.

Today An Old Man Died

Time does not pause in recognition,

But merely makes a ripple

On the surface of its sea,

Because today an old man died.

There was scarcely a journalistic note:

"He was eighty three."

Where is the work of four score years?

Where is the loving care?

Unnoted

By cold and hurrying society,

But well remembered with honor and love

By those who called him

Dad.

To My Grieving Friend

With eyes wept dry,

While tears run in rivulets

Inside my heart,

I look upon your grief

Helplessly.

Only reaching out my hand

To make you know I love you,

And I am here.

An Offering of Sympathy

I weep with you,

But to really feel your sorrow,

My friend,

Within my imagination, I too, must lose a son.

So, I cannot comprehend your loss,

~~Because~~

My heart staggers away from such imagining,

While for you it is reality.

Please understand, my friend,

I can only offer tears

And love.

Yesterday

Yesterday

We began our life and love together.

In faith,

Our eyes were on tomorrow,

Full of dreams.

How quickly tomorrow has become

Today!

And is slipping away into

Yesterday.

Gallery

I know your face

Apart from all those faces

Lined upon the wall

Of my memory.

Some are drawn with familiar lines

Of association,

Some with warm affection.

Your dear face is deeply etched

With perfect similitude

In love.

Seven Wasted Tears

While you were gone

I wept seven tears in my loneliness,

Or was it seventy times seven?

Count them!

But how can you count a sodden pillow?

Oh, wastefulness!

For then I smiled a thousand smiles

At the end of loneliness.

Seven wasted tears.

Reunion

Memories

Of faces, and voices, and ways of being

Stored upon the shelves

Of the storehouse of my mind.

Forgotten,

Until this day,

Then recalled into the light of now.

A changed facade of greying hair,

And wrinkled brow

Has not altered the bad we were,

Or the good,

But God uses time to cleanse the mind

And heart

Of all but love.

So we delight in reunion.

A Very Special Day

Even with the dawn,

It seemed

That I could breathe the beauty of the day

Into my soul.

The breeze whispered tidings

Of contentment,

And hearts received the message.

The hours fit themselves around my will to do,

Or not.

It was a day to spend

Like money saved for a special time,

So I spent the day

In happiness.

Empty Shells

I could not help but stand in awe

Of dereliction when I saw

The house, one time a lovely home.

So silent, waiting as for some

Departed song of life to come.

But now too late, so still and cold

An empty shell without a soul.

The life of man is so like this,

With strong and stately edifice.

But then with true synonymy,

The breath departs, we yearn to see

Returning of vitality.

But now too late, so still and cold

An empty shell without a soul.

Memories

Memories,

Whispering with gossipy tongues,

Drift through my mind,

Whispering stories

Of small boys, Christmas, snowfall,

And bright sunny summer days;

Of days that ring with laughter,

And other days, remembered with tears.

In derisive tones,

They tell of dismal failures,

And I frantically search their tales to find

Perhaps one plaudit for my ego.

No matter.

What they really have to tell about

Is happiness.